ELI TOMAC

The Boy Who Conquered the Dirt

A MOTORCYCLE BIOGRAPHY FOR KIDS

Sherry L. Proffitt

All rights reserved. No part of this publication may be reproduced, distributed, or transmitted in any form or by any means, including photocopying, recording, or other electronic or mechanical methods, without the prior written permission of the publisher, except in the case of brief quotations embodied in critical reviews and certain other noncommercial uses permitted by copyright law.

Copyright © Sherry L. Proffitt, 2025

INTRODCUTION	**6**
CHAPTER 1: A FUTURE CHAMPION IS BORN	**10**
A Racing Family Legacy	10
Welcome to the World	16
CHAPTER 2: THE EARLY YEARS ON TWO WHEELS	**22**
CHAPTER 3: RISING THROUGH THE AMATEUR RANKS	**28**
The Big Break	35
CHAPTER 4: TURNING PRO – A STAR IS BORN	**40**
CHAPTER 5: THE 450CC TRANSITION – BIGGER, FASTER, TOUGHER	**46**
CHAPTER 6: THE CHAMPIONSHIP YEARS	**50**
CHAPTER 7: THE RIVALRIES AND COMEBACKS	**58**
CHAPTER 8: SWITCHING TEAMS	**64**
A New Chapter	64
CHAPTER 9: RECORDS, ACHIEVEMENTS, AND LEGACY	**68**
Eli's Place in Motocross History	68
A Hero for Young Riders	75
CHAPTER 10: LIFE BEYOND THE TRACK	**78**

CHAPTER 11: THE FUTURE OF ELI TOMAC	**84**
🏁 Fᴜɴ Fᴀᴄᴛs Aʙᴏᴜᴛ Eʟɪ Tᴏᴍᴀᴄ 🏁	90
🏍 Fᴜɴ Fᴀᴄᴛs Aʙᴏᴜᴛ Mᴏᴛᴏʀᴄʏᴄʟᴇs ᴛᴏ Bʟᴏᴡ Yᴏᴜʀ Mɪɴᴅ! 🏍	95
Eʟɪ's Fᴀᴠᴏʀɪᴛᴇ Tʀᴀᴄᴋs ᴀɴᴅ Rᴀᴄᴇs	99
🏍 Mᴏᴛᴏᴄʀᴏss Tᴇʀᴍs Exᴘʟᴀɪɴᴇᴅ ғᴏʀ Yᴏᴜɴɢ Rᴇᴀᴅᴇʀs! 🏍	106
CONCLUSION	**114**

INTRODCUTION

There's something magical about the way a dirt bike roars to life. The loud vroom-vroom of the engine, the smell of fresh dirt being kicked into the air, and the wind rushing past as the bike soars over jumps. It's a feeling that makes hearts race, palms sweat, and eyes widen with excitement. But for one boy, this wasn't just a feeling—it was his life. His name is Eli Tomac, and he didn't just ride dirt bikes; he conquered the dirt.

Imagine gripping the handlebars of a powerful motorcycle, feeling the ground shake beneath you, and twisting the throttle to blast off like a rocket. The track is rough, full of bumps and turns that could send even the best riders tumbling. But not Eli. He wasn't afraid of the dirt. He loved it. He chased it, battled it, and made it his own. From the moment he first climbed onto a bike, he knew this wasn't just a sport—this was his adventure.

But let's get one thing straight. Eli Tomac wasn't handed a golden ticket to success. He didn't just wake up one morning and become one of the fastest motocross racers in the world. No, Eli had to earn it. He had to practice until his legs ached, his arms felt like jelly, and his heart pounded like a drum. He had to get up every time he fell—and he fell a lot. Dirt bikes don't care if you're tired. They don't care if you're having a bad day. They challenge you, push you, and sometimes, they throw you straight into the ground. But Eli never let that stop him.

Picture a young boy, no older than you, strapping on his helmet, adjusting his gloves, and rolling his dirt bike onto a track full of riders bigger, stronger, and more experienced than him. Some kids might have been nervous. Some might have doubted themselves. But Eli? He was ready. He lined up at the starting gate, his heart pounding like the engine beneath him. The countdown began. Three... two... one... Boom! The gate dropped, and just like that, the race was on!

Dirt flew into the air as the bikes tore down the track. Eli leaned into the turns, gripping his handlebars tighter with every twist and jump. He wasn't the biggest kid on the track. He wasn't the oldest. But he had something special—fearlessness. Every jump he cleared, every turn he nailed, every race he finished made him stronger. He wasn't just riding—he was learning. He was training for something bigger.

But racing isn't just about speed. It's about determination. It's about getting up when you crash, even when it hurts. It's about facing the biggest, toughest riders in the world and saying, I belong here. And that's exactly what Eli did. He kept training, kept racing, and kept pushing himself until he wasn't just another rider in the pack—he was the rider to beat.

As he grew older, the tracks got bigger, the races got harder, and the competition got fiercer. Some days, he won. Some days, he lost. But every time he put on his helmet, he gave it everything he had. Because that's what champions do. They don't quit. They don't give up. They ride faster, train harder, and chase their dreams until they catch them.

And that's how Eli Tomac became one of the greatest motocross racers in history. His journey wasn't easy, and it wasn't always fun. But through every bump, every bruise, and every battle with the dirt, he proved one thing—he was born to ride.

So, if you've ever dreamed of doing something big, something exciting, something that makes your heart race like an engine at the starting line—this book is for you. Because Eli Tomac's story isn't just about riding motorcycles. It's about never giving up. It's about chasing what you love, even when it's tough. And most of all, it's about believing in yourself.

Now, get ready to hit the gas and hold on tight—because this is the incredible story of the boy who conquered the dirt.

Chapter 1: A Future Champion is Born

A Racing Family Legacy

The sound of engines has been part of the Tomac family for a long, long time. Before Eli Tomac became one of the fastest motocross racers in the world, before he was flying over dirt jumps and racing to championships, there was another Tomac who knew all about speed. His name was John Tomac, and he wasn't just any racer—he was a legend in the world of mountain biking.

Now, let's imagine something. Picture a young boy, not Eli this time, but someone else. This boy wasn't racing dirt bikes, but he was just as fearless, just as determined, and just as fast. His world wasn't filled with revving motocross engines, but with the smooth hum of bicycle tires rolling over dirt trails and rocky paths. That boy was Eli's dad, John Tomac, and his story begins way before Eli was even born.

John Tomac was born on November 3, 1967, in a small town called Owosso, in the state of Michigan, USA. If you had met John as a kid, you would have seen a boy who never sat still. He was always moving, always riding, always looking for the next adventure. Some kids liked playing with toys. Some liked drawing or reading. But John? He loved the feeling of the wind rushing past his face, the thrill of going fast, and the excitement of pushing himself further than before.

By the time John was a teenager, bicycles weren't just for fun anymore—they were a way of life. He started racing BMX bikes in the early 1980s, competing in fast-paced, high-flying races that took place on dirt tracks filled with jumps, turns, and obstacles. BMX racing was all about speed, skill, and bravery, and John had plenty of all three. He wasn't just good—he was incredible.

But John wasn't the kind of person who stayed in one place for too long. He was always looking for a new challenge, a new way to test himself. So, as he grew older, he switched from BMX racing to something even bigger—mountain biking. This was a sport where riders had to race over rough trails, climb steep hills, and speed down rocky mountainsides. It was tough. It was dangerous. And it was exactly what John loved.

In the late 1980s, mountain biking was still a new sport, but John wasn't afraid to take it on. In 1988, at just 21 years old, he joined a professional team and started competing in races all over the country. But John didn't just want to be another racer—he wanted to be the best. And he was.

Between 1988 and the mid-1990s, John Tomac became one of the greatest mountain bikers the world had ever seen. He won multiple national and world championships, proving that he could race with the best and come out on top. He didn't just stick to one type of racing, either. He was a champion in cross-country races, which tested a rider's endurance and speed over long distances, and downhill racing, where riders had to race down steep mountains as fast as possible. No one could stop him.

But John wasn't only a mountain biker. He was a racer through and through. He even competed in road cycling, riding on smooth pavement with some of the fastest cyclists in the world. In 1991, he raced in the Tour de France, the most famous road cycling race in history! Imagine that—one man competing in BMX, mountain biking, and road cycling at the highest level. That's how incredible John Tomac was.

Now, let's take a moment to think about something. How does one become a champion? Some people might say talent. Some might say speed. But the truth is, being a champion is about hard work. It's about waking up every day, training, practicing, and never giving up—even when things get tough. That's exactly what John did. He trained harder than anyone else. He rode his bike for hours and hours, day after day, week after week, year after year. He fell. He crashed. He got hurt. But he never quit.

And that's an important part of this story. Because if you know anything about Eli Tomac, you know that he never quits either. That mindset, that never-give-up attitude? He got that from his dad.

But here's the thing about being an athlete—it's not just about winning. It's about loving the sport, about pushing yourself to be better, and about sharing that passion with others. And that's exactly what John did. Even after he had won championship after championship, after he had become one of the biggest names in mountain biking, he never lost his love for racing. He wanted to share that love with the next generation.

That's why, in the late 1990s, John and his wife Kathy Tomac moved to a quiet place in Cortez, Colorado. They didn't move to a big city or a fancy neighborhood. They moved to the wide-open countryside, a place with rolling hills, dusty trails, and miles of land perfect for riding. It wasn't just a home—it was a training ground. It was a place where a future champion could grow up, ride, and learn what it truly meant to be a racer.

Now, let's pause for a second. Because this is where the story gets even more interesting. Some people think that racing is just about the rider—the one on the bike, the one crossing the finish line. But that's not true. Racing is about family. It's about the people who support you, train with you, push you to be better, and believe in you even when you doubt yourself.

John Tomac knew exactly what it meant to be a racer. He had been through the tough races, the injuries, the victories, and the defeats. He knew what it felt like to stand on top of the podium, and he knew what it felt like to fall and have to get back up. He had learned every lesson that racing could teach. And he wasn't going to keep those lessons to himself. He was going to pass them on.

But who would he pass them on to? Who would be the one to take that knowledge, that love of speed, that determination to be great?

Well, if you've been paying attention, you already know the answer.

Because soon, there would be another Tomac who loved to go fast. Another Tomac who wanted to race. Another Tomac who had that same fire in his heart—the same passion, the same drive.

But before we get to him, before we talk about his journey, we need to understand this: Eli Tomac didn't just wake up one day and decide to be a racer. He was born into a family that lived for racing. A family that knew what it meant to train hard, to dream big, and to never back down from a challenge.

And so, on that quiet land in Cortez, Colorado, with dirt trails winding through the hills and the sun shining down on the wide-open space, the next chapter of the Tomac racing story was about to begin.

But that's a story for another time. Because for now, all you need to know is this: before Eli Tomac ever raced a single lap, before he ever gripped the handlebars of a dirt bike, there was a legacy—a racing family legacy.

And that legacy started with a man named John Tomac, a man who conquered the mountains before his son conquered the dirt.

Welcome to the World

There are moments in life that change everything. Moments that seem small at first but grow into something incredible. Moments that create champions, dreamers, and legends. And on November 14, 1992, in a small town called Cortez, Colorado, one of those moments happened.

It wasn't a loud moment. There were no roaring engines, no speeding bikes, no crowds cheering. Just the quiet hum of a hospital room, the soft voices of doctors and nurses, and the joyful, nervous excitement of two parents waiting to meet their new baby. And then, just like that, he was here. Eli Tomac had entered the world.

The world didn't know it yet, but something special had just begun. Because this wasn't just any baby. This wasn't just another boy who would grow up, go to school, and follow an ordinary path. No, this baby was different. His story would be filled with adventure, speed, and dirt flying through the air. His life would be about racing, about pushing limits, about becoming one of the fastest motocross riders the world had ever seen.

But at that moment, in that hospital room, he was just Eli, a tiny baby with bright eyes and a strong heart. His parents, John and Kathy Tomac, looked at him with love, holding him close, wondering who he would become.

John knew something about greatness. He had been a champion himself, racing on two wheels, speeding through trails, conquering mountains, and winning world championships. But as he looked at his newborn son, he wasn't thinking about trophies or racing. He was thinking about family. Because family always came first.

Cortez, Colorado, wasn't like big cities filled with busy streets and noisy traffic. It was quiet, peaceful, surrounded by wide-open land, rolling hills, and endless skies. It was the kind of place where a boy could grow up strong and wild, where adventure was always waiting just outside the door.

From the very start, Eli was a curious and energetic little boy. He wasn't the kind of baby who just sat still and watched the world. No, he wanted to explore. He wanted to move. He wanted to see everything. As soon as he could crawl, he was off—zipping across the floor, grabbing onto things, eager to go, go, go.

And once he could walk? Oh, there was no stopping him.

Most toddlers play with stuffed animals or toy blocks. But Eli? He had something else—tiny toy motorcycles.

Before he could even talk, he would grab those little bikes, roll them across the floor, making vroom-vroom noises with his mouth. He didn't just like bikes. He loved them. There was something about the way they moved, the way they looked, the way they sounded.

But where did this love come from? Was it just in his heart from the start? Or was there something—someone—that inspired him?

The answer, of course, was his dad.

John Tomac had spent his life on two wheels, racing at high speeds, winning championships, and pushing himself to be the best. And though Eli was still just a little boy, he could already see how amazing his dad was.

Imagine being a small child, watching your father race across a track, jumping high into the air, landing smoothly, and speeding past the finish line. Imagine seeing him train every day, pushing himself harder, never giving up. Imagine the sound of the tires gripping the dirt, the roar of the engines, the cheers from the crowd.

For some kids, racing might have just been something to watch. But for Eli, it was something else. It was magic.

His house wasn't like other houses. While some kids had backyards filled with swing sets and soccer balls, Eli's backyard was filled with bikes, gear, helmets, and dirt trails.

Racing wasn't just something that happened on TV. It was right there, all around him, every single day.

Eli would sit in the garage and watch his dad work on bikes, fixing them, tuning them, getting them ready to race. He would listen as John talked about strategy, speed, and control. He would see the trophies lined up on the shelves, shining reminders of how much hard work it took to win.

And every time he saw his dad ride, every time he watched the wheels spin and the dirt fly, something inside of him sparked.

It was passion.

He might not have known the word yet. He might not have been able to explain what he was feeling. But it was there, deep inside him, growing stronger every day.

He wanted to ride.

He wanted to feel the wind in his face, the power of the bike beneath him, the excitement of the race.

He didn't just want to watch his dad. He wanted to be like him.

But here's something important. No one ever forced Eli to love bikes. No one ever told him, You have to race. No one ever said, This is what you must do.

That's not how passion works.

Passion is something you feel. It's something that calls to you, something that makes your heart beat faster, something that makes you excited to wake up every morning and do what you love.

And for Eli, that passion was already burning inside him.

Everywhere he went, he imagined himself racing. When he ran across the yard, he wasn't just running—he was pretending to be on a bike, speeding through a track, winning a race. When he played with his toy motorcycles, he wasn't just playing—he was dreaming, picturing himself on a real bike, twisting the throttle, zooming across the dirt.

There was no question about it.

Eli Tomac belonged on two wheels.

He wasn't just a kid who liked bikes. He was a kid who was meant to ride.

And soon—sooner than anyone could have imagined—he wouldn't just be dreaming about it.

He would be riding.

Because his first real bike was coming.

And once he climbed on, there would be no turning back.

Chapter 2: The Early Years on Two Wheels

The day Eli Tomac got his first dirt bike was a day that changed everything. It wasn't just any birthday or any ordinary gift. It was the moment when his dreams became real. It was the moment when the dirt, the speed, the thrill—all of it—became more than something he imagined. Now, he could finally ride.

Eli had spent years watching, waiting, and dreaming. He had seen his dad, John Tomac, train, race, and win. He had sat on the sidelines, wishing he could feel the rush of the wind, the power of the engine, the thrill of the ride. And then, at just three years old, that moment finally came.

It was a tiny dirt bike, the perfect size for a little boy with big dreams. It wasn't too fast, but to Eli, it felt like a rocket. His parents had given it to him, knowing that their little boy was meant to ride. Some kids get bicycles with training wheels. Eli got a motorcycle with a real engine, real speed, and real dirt waiting for him.

The first time he climbed onto the bike, his feet barely touched the ground. The handlebars felt huge in his tiny hands. But there was no hesitation. No fear. He gripped the handles, twisted the throttle, and the bike rumbled to life. His heart raced, and his face lit up with excitement. This was it. This was what he had been waiting for.

Of course, learning to ride a dirt bike wasn't as easy as playing with toy motorcycles on the floor. The first few times, he wobbled. He leaned too much on one side. He tipped over. But every time he fell, he got back up, dusted off his little riding suit, and tried again.

And again.

And again.

Until, one day, he didn't fall.

One day, he zoomed across the yard, kicking up tiny clouds of dust, his little legs gripping the bike tight, his hands steady on the handlebars. He wasn't just riding. He was flying.

He rode through the open fields near his home, twisting and turning, getting faster and braver with every ride. He rode over bumps, through trails, over tiny hills. And every time, he went a little faster, leaned a little harder, felt a little stronger.

Riding wasn't just something Eli did. It was who he was.

By the time he was four years old, he wasn't just riding in his backyard anymore. His dad had built small practice tracks for him, places where he could start learning the real skills of motocross—cornering, jumping, balancing, and controlling speed. Some kids were still riding tricycles at four years old. Eli? He was already becoming a racer.

At first, his rides were just for fun. But it didn't take long before fun turned into competition. Eli wanted to race. He didn't just want to ride in circles. He wanted to line up at the start gate, hear the countdown, and go full speed against other kids.

And so, at just seven years old, Eli entered his very first motocross race.

The track was bigger than anything he had ever ridden before. The dirt was rough, the turns were sharp, and the jumps looked huge. He wasn't just riding for fun now—he was racing against other kids who were just as fast, just as hungry to win. The starting gate dropped, and his heart pounded like an engine. He gripped the handlebars, twisted the throttle, and launched forward.

At first, he wasn't the fastest. Some of the other riders had more experience, more confidence. But Eli didn't give up. He pushed harder, rode smarter, and by the time he crossed the finish line, he wasn't just another rider—he was a competitor.

He didn't win his first race. But he did something just as important. He proved to himself that he could do it.

That first race was just the beginning. By the time he was eight years old, Eli was racing all over the country. He started competing in amateur motocross championships, where kids from all over came to race, to battle for trophies, and to prove who was the best.

And guess what?

Eli wasn't just another kid on the track anymore. He was winning.

He trained harder than ever, waking up early to ride, practicing for hours every single day. Some kids played video games after school. Eli practiced jumps, sharp turns, and high-speed straights.

Some kids spent weekends watching cartoons. Eli spent his weekends at motocross tracks, racing against the fastest young riders in the country.

And he was getting better. Faster. Stronger.

And he had a secret weapon—his dad.

John Tomac wasn't a motocross racer, but he knew everything about racing. He knew about speed, control, endurance, and mental strength. He knew what it took to win. He had won world championships in mountain biking. He had trained harder than anyone. He had faced the toughest competitions, the hardest courses, and the biggest challenges.

And now, he was passing all of that knowledge to Eli.

John didn't just teach Eli how to go fast. He taught him how to race smart.

How to read the track.

How to take the best racing lines.

How to handle pressure when there were other riders all around him, trying to take the lead.

How to keep going, even when his body was tired, even when the race was tough.

Some kids had coaches. Eli had a father who was also a champion.

And it made all the difference.

Eli listened, trained harder, and kept pushing himself. He didn't just want to be good. He wanted to be the best.

By the time he was 10 years old, he was winning national amateur championships. People were starting to talk about him. They saw the way he rode, the way he handled his bike, the way he never backed down from a challenge.

"He's going to be something special," they said.

And they were right.

Eli's journey wasn't just about talent. It was about work. About heart. About never giving up.

And it all started with that little dirt bike when he was just three years old.

It started with those first wobbly rides, those tiny crashes, those big dreams.

It started with that first race at seven years old, where he learned that even if you don't win, you get back up and try again.

It started with every single lesson his dad taught him, every piece of advice, every push to be better.

Eli wasn't just another kid with a dirt bike.

He was a racer.

And he was just getting started.

Chapter 3: Rising Through the Amateur Ranks

Eli Tomac had never been the kind of kid who liked to sit still. From the moment he got his first dirt bike, he was always moving, always riding, always looking for the next challenge. He wasn't just a boy who liked motorcycles—he was a boy who wanted to race. And not just race for fun. He wanted to win.

Winning wasn't easy. It never is. But Eli had something special—determination. Some kids try a sport, struggle a little, and decide to quit. But not Eli. Every time he lost a race, he trained harder. Every time he fell, he got back up. And that's how he went from a little boy riding in his backyard to a racer competing on the biggest amateur motocross tracks in the country.

It all started with local races. These were smaller events, usually held at tracks near his home in Colorado. They weren't big championships with cameras and crowds. But to Eli, every race mattered. Every race was a chance to learn, improve, and prove himself.

At just seven years old, he was already competing in real motocross races. The kids he raced against weren't just riding for fun—they wanted to win, too. The competition was tough, but Eli pushed himself harder than ever. He didn't always win, but he always learned.

Then, something started happening. Eli began winning—a lot.

One by one, he started beating the other kids. His speed got better, his jumps got higher, his turns got sharper. He was no longer just "that fast kid from Colorado"—he was becoming a real threat on the track.

As he won more local races, people started noticing. Who was this kid? How was he getting so fast? The motocross world was always looking for the next big star, and some people were starting to whisper that Eli Tomac just might be it.

Winning small races was exciting, but Eli wanted more. He wanted to race against the best young riders in the country. And that meant competing for amateur motocross titles.

Now, what is an amateur motocross title?

An amateur title is what a racer wins before they become a professional. Think of it like a championship for young riders. Before someone can race in the biggest pro events, they have to prove themselves in the amateur ranks. These races bring together the best young racers from all over the country. Winning an amateur title isn't just about getting a trophy—it's about showing the world that you're one of the best.

And that's exactly what Eli did.

He started entering national amateur motocross events, where only the best young racers were invited to compete. These races weren't just for fun anymore. They were serious. The kids who won these races would be the future stars of the sport. And Eli? He wasn't just there to race. He was there to win.

By the time Eli was 10 years old, he had already won multiple amateur motocross titles.

His name was everywhere in the amateur motocross world. People knew that he was fast. They knew that he had incredible control over his bike. But most of all, they knew that he had something even more important—the heart of a champion.

But how did he do it?

How did Eli go from a kid racing on small local tracks to a national amateur champion?

The answer was simple: training, discipline, and dedication.

Eli didn't just wake up one morning and decide to be great. He worked for it—every single day.

His training wasn't easy. Some kids spend their afternoons watching TV or playing video games. Eli? He was on the track, practicing for hours and hours.

He woke up early. Even when he was tired.

He trained in the heat. Even when the sun was burning down.

He rode in the cold. Even when his fingers felt frozen.

He practiced turning, jumping, landing, speeding up, slowing down—every tiny detail that could make him a better racer.

Because in motocross, the difference between winning and losing can be just a few seconds.

Eli's dad, John Tomac, played a huge role in his training. John had been a world champion in mountain biking, and he knew exactly what it took to be the best.

But here's something interesting—John never forced Eli to train.

Some parents push their kids into sports, making them practice all the time, even if they don't want to. But not John. He wanted Eli to love racing, not feel like it was a job.

So instead of pushing him too hard, he let Eli set his own pace.

And Eli? He wanted to train. He wanted to be better.

Because Eli didn't just love winning. He loved riding.

John taught Eli everything he knew about racing. He helped Eli learn how to take the best lines through corners, how to stay calm under pressure, and how to think like a champion.

One of the biggest lessons John taught Eli was that racing isn't just about speed—it's about strategy.

A great racer doesn't just twist the throttle and go as fast as possible. A great racer is smart.

They know when to push harder and when to hold back.

They know how to save energy for the final laps of a race.

They know how to read the track, finding the fastest and safest path.

And Eli? He listened.

He soaked up every piece of advice his dad gave him. He trained his body and his mind. He learned how to stay focused, how to stay strong, and how to never, ever give up.

And that's why he kept winning.

That's why, by the time he was 12 years old, he wasn't just another amateur rider—he was one of the best young racers in the country.

His name was in magazines. His face was on motocross websites. People knew that Eli Tomac was a rising star.

But there was still more work to do.

Because winning in the amateur ranks was only the beginning.

Eli had his eyes on something even bigger.

He didn't just want to be a great amateur racer.

He wanted to go pro.

And to do that, he had to keep training, keep improving, and keep proving that he was ready for the next level.

Because in the world of motocross, only the strongest, fastest, and most determined riders make it to the top.

And Eli Tomac?

He was on his way.

The Big Break

There are moments in life that change everything. Moments that take someone from being just another racer to being a name people will never forget. For Eli Tomac, that moment happened at Loretta Lynn's Championship, the biggest amateur motocross race in the world.

Eli had already been racing for years. He had won local races, he had competed in national amateur events, and he had proven that he was fast. But in the world of motocross, being fast isn't always enough. To become a real star, a rider has to do something big. Something that makes everyone sit up, take notice, and say, "Wow, this kid is special."

And that's exactly what happened when Eli raced at Loretta Lynn's.

Now, what is Loretta Lynn's Championship?

It's not just any race. It's the biggest and most important amateur motocross race in the country. Every young rider in America dreams of racing there because it's the place where future motocross legends are made.

Winning at Loretta Lynn's means everything.

This championship is named after Loretta Lynn, a famous country music singer who owned a huge ranch in Hurricane Mills, Tennessee. The ranch had lots of land, hills, and dirt—the perfect place for a motocross track. In 1982, the first-ever Amateur National Motocross Championship was held there, and over the years, it became the most famous amateur motocross event in the world.

To even get to Loretta Lynn's, a rider has to qualify. It's not like a regular race where anyone can sign up. Thousands of kids try out, but only the fastest make it. The ones who do get to race on a national stage, in front of big motocross teams, sponsors, and even professional riders.

In 2010, at just 17 years old, Eli Tomac lined up at Loretta Lynn's, ready to prove himself to the world.

This was the biggest race of his life.

The starting gate was packed with the fastest amateur riders in the country. These weren't just kids racing for fun—they were all chasing the dream of turning pro. Some of them had been racing since they were toddlers, just like Eli. Some of them had already won big races. All of them wanted to win this championship.

The track was rough and challenging. The Tennessee heat made the dirt dry and dusty, and every time the bikes roared around the track, clouds of dust filled the air. The jumps were big. The turns were sharp. Only the best riders would survive.

Eli wasn't nervous. He was ready.

The crowd was buzzing. Fans, families, and motocross teams all watched from the sidelines, waiting to see who would rise above the rest. This was the race that had launched so many motocross stars—Ricky Carmichael, James Stewart, Ryan Villopoto, Travis Pastrana—all of them had won here before going pro. Eli wanted to be next.

The gate dropped.

The engines roared.

And the race began.

Eli's bike shot forward, kicking up dirt as he raced into the first turn. He was surrounded by riders, all of them fighting for the lead. Elbows bumped. Tires skidded. The sound of engines filled the air.

But Eli was locked in.

Lap after lap, he pushed himself harder than ever. He took the inside lines on the corners, making sharp turns without losing speed. He hit the jumps with perfect precision, landing smoothly and getting back on the gas without hesitation.

Every second counted. Every tiny mistake could mean losing the race.

One rider was ahead of him. That wasn't going to last.

Eli picked up speed, his focus sharper than ever. He wasn't just riding—he was flying. He cut through the rough sections, his bike staying steady while others bounced and lost control.

Then, with just a few laps left, he saw his chance.

He moved to the inside on a tight corner, made his move, and passed the leader.

The crowd erupted.

Eli was in the lead.

Now, all he had to do was hold onto it.

The final laps felt like forever. His arms were burning. His legs were sore. But he didn't slow down. He didn't let anyone catch him. He knew this was his moment.

And then—

He crossed the finish line.

First place.

Champion.

Eli Tomac had won Loretta Lynn's.

The crowd cheered. His family hugged each other. His dad smiled proudly. Eli had just proven that he was ready for something bigger.

This wasn't just another win. This was his big break.

Because winning at Loretta Lynn's meant the motocross world was watching.

Winning at Loretta Lynn's meant professional teams were paying attention.

Winning at Loretta Lynn's meant Eli Tomac was about to go pro.

And from that day on, nothing would ever be the same.

Chapter 4: Turning Pro – A Star is Born

There are moments in life when everything changes. One day, you're just a kid chasing dreams, and the next, you're standing on the biggest stage, facing the toughest competition, ready to prove that you belong. For Eli Tomac, that moment came when he stepped into the professional motocross scene.

Becoming a professional isn't something that happens overnight. It takes years of hard work, endless practice, and countless races to get noticed. But Eli had done it all. He had won races, dominated in amateur competitions, and made a name for himself as one of the fastest young riders in motocross. He had trained harder than ever, spending hours on the track, learning every jump, every turn, every strategy that could make him a champion.

And finally, in 2010, at just 17 years old, it was time.

Eli was about to race in his first professional motocross season.

Now, let's pause for a second. What does it mean to go pro?

For a motocross rider, turning professional means racing against the best riders in the world. It means no more amateur events, no more small races. Every race would now be on the biggest tracks, with the fastest riders, under the brightest lights.

It was a huge step.

And Eli? He was ready.

His first professional race was at the Hangtown Motocross Classic, one of the most famous motocross events in the world. This race had been around for decades, and only the best riders competed here. Fans filled the stands. Cameras were everywhere. The roar of engines echoed across the track.

Eli lined up at the starting gate, his heart pounding with excitement. The other riders around him were professionals, men who had been racing at this level for years. They were stronger, more experienced, and ready to test the new kid.

The gate dropped.

The race began.

And something incredible happened.

Eli won.

Not just a good race. He won his very first professional race.

Nobody expected it. Nobody thought a rookie, a kid racing his very first pro event, could beat the best riders in the world. But Eli didn't care about expectations. He didn't care that he was young. He just raced.

And he won.

It was a historic moment. Eli Tomac became the first rider in history to win his professional debut in the 250cc class. No other rider had ever done it before.

But what is the 250cc class, and why does it matter?

In motocross, different bikes are used for different races. The 250cc class is where young professional riders compete before moving to the bigger 450cc class. Think of it as the first step in the pro ranks—the place where new stars are born.

And Eli? He wasn't just in the 250cc class. He dominated it.

After winning his debut race, he didn't stop. He kept racing, kept winning, kept proving that he was one of the best. He had speed, skill, and the kind of focus that made every single lap count.

Fans couldn't believe it.

Other racers couldn't believe it.

Eli Tomac was no longer just a fast kid from Colorado.

He was a rising motocross star.

And people were watching. Big people. Important people. People who sponsor riders.

Now, let's talk about something exciting—factory support and sponsorships.

What does this mean?

Imagine you're a young athlete, and you're so good that the biggest sports brands in the world want to help you. They give you the best gear, the best bikes, and everything you need to win.

That's what happened to Eli.

Because he was winning so many races, big motocross teams wanted him. These teams were sponsored by companies that made the fastest bikes, the best riding gear, and the top equipment in the world.

And soon, Eli had something every young rider dreams of—a factory ride.

A factory ride means that a big motocross company gives a rider their best bike, best mechanics, and full support to help them win. It's like being on a professional sports team, with everything you need to be the best.

Eli joined Geico Honda, one of the most famous motocross teams at the time.

This was huge.

Now, Eli wasn't just racing on his own. He had a full team behind him—mechanics, trainers, and sponsors who believed in him. He had a Honda factory bike, a machine built for speed, power, and championships.

This changed everything.

With his new bike, new team, and new professional mindset, Eli was unstoppable.

He didn't just compete in the 250cc class. He dominated it.

He won race after race, showing that he wasn't just a lucky rookie—he was the real deal.

Motocross fans started chanting his name. "Tomac! Tomac! Tomac!"

Other riders knew they had to watch out.

Because Eli Tomac wasn't just fast.

He was a champion in the making.

And this was only the beginning.

Chapter 5: The 450cc Transition – Bigger, Faster, Tougher

Eli Tomac had already proven himself as a champion in the 250cc class. He had won races, battled against some of the fastest young riders, and shown the world that he was more than just a rising star—he was the future of motocross. But in the world of racing, the journey never stops. There's always a bigger challenge, a tougher battle, a new mountain to climb.

For Eli, that next challenge was the 450cc class—the Premier Class of motocross.

Now, what does that even mean?

Let's think about it like this: imagine you're playing in the biggest, most important soccer league in the world. The games are faster. The players are stronger. The competition is tougher. That's what moving to the 450cc class is like in motocross.

The 450cc class is where the best of the best race. The bikes are bigger, more powerful, and harder to control. The riders have more experience, more strength, and more speed. In the 250cc class, Eli had raced against some of the fastest young riders in the world. But in 450cc? He would be racing against legends.

This was the class where champions were made.

The class where motocross history was written.

The class where only the strongest riders survived.

And Eli? He was ready to prove that he belonged.

But moving to the 450cc class wasn't easy.

These bikes were bigger, faster, and more dangerous. They had more power, which meant Eli had to learn how to control his bike in a completely new way. He had to adjust to the speed, the weight, and the brutal competition.

In 2014, Eli made his 450cc debut, stepping onto the track with the greatest motocross riders of his time.

And who were these legends?

There was Ryan Dungey, a multi-time champion known for his consistency and smart racing. He didn't make mistakes, and he was always one of the toughest riders to beat.

Then there was Ken Roczen, a German superstar with unbelievable speed and skill. Roczen had already won big races in both Europe and the U.S., and he was a major competitor in the 450cc class.

And of course, there was Chad Reed, one of the most experienced and respected riders in motocross history. He had been racing at the top level for years and was known for his toughness and never-give-up attitude.

These riders weren't just good—they were great. They had won championships, set records, and built legacies in the sport.

And now, Eli was racing against them.

The pressure was high. The expectations were huge. Some people thought it would take years before Eli could really compete with these legends.

But Eli didn't believe in waiting.

He was ready to fight right away.

His first year in 450cc was tough. There were crashes. There were injuries. There were races where things didn't go as planned. He learned the hard way that this class was a completely different level.

But every time he fell, he got back up. Every race was a lesson. Every lap made him better, stronger, and more prepared.

And then, something amazing happened.

In 2015, Eli won his first big 450cc race.

It was at the Thunder Valley National, a legendary outdoor motocross race held in Colorado. His home state.

The track was rough. The competition was fierce. The race was one of the toughest of the season. But Eli was unstoppable.

Lap after lap, he rode with confidence and power. He didn't just keep up with the legends—he beat them.

He raced past Dungey, Roczen, and Reed.

He hit the jumps higher and faster than ever before.

He handled the corners with perfect precision.

And when he crossed the finish line, he was first place.

The crowd exploded. His team cheered. His dad watched proudly.

Eli Tomac had done it.

He had won his first big race in the 450cc class.

This wasn't just a victory. This was proof.

Proof that he belonged with the best.

Proof that he was ready to fight for championships.

Proof that Eli Tomac wasn't just another rider—he was a future legend.

And from that moment on, he was no longer just competing in the 450cc class.

He was dominating it.

And this?

This was only the beginning.

Chapter 6: The Championship Years

Eli Tomac had already climbed so many mountains in his motocross career. He had raced in local events, won amateur championships, turned pro, and battled against the best riders in the world. But there was still more to conquer. There were still bigger races, tougher competitions, and new challenges waiting for him.

Because in the world of motorcycle racing, there are two massive championships that every rider dreams of winning—Supercross and Motocross.

But what exactly are Supercross and Motocross?

To understand how Eli became a champion, we first have to understand what these races really are.

Motocross is the original, classic form of dirt bike racing. It takes place outdoors, on natural terrain, with long tracks full of huge jumps, deep ruts, and unpredictable conditions. The races are tough. They happen in mud, rain, dust, and heat. The riders have to battle through every kind of weather and race on tracks that change every single lap.

Supercross, on the other hand, is like Motocross's flashy cousin. It's held indoors, in huge stadiums, where thousands of fans pack the seats and cheer as the riders fly through the air. The tracks are tight, technical, and full of crazy jumps. The races are shorter, but the action is nonstop.

Winning in both Supercross and Motocross is one of the hardest things a rider can do. It takes speed, skill, endurance, and absolute fearlessness.

And guess what?

Eli Tomac didn't just compete in these races. He dominated them.

Over the years, Eli fought his way to the top of the sport. He went up against the fastest riders, the toughest conditions, and the biggest challenges. He didn't win every race—but he never gave up.

And one by one, he started stacking up titles.

He won Motocross Nationals.

He won Supercross Main Events.

And by 2020, he was one of the biggest names in motocross.

But 2020 wasn't an easy year.

In fact, it was one of the hardest years of his career.

That year, Eli was chasing his first-ever Supercross Championship. Even though he had already won many races, the one thing missing from his career was the big Supercross title. He had come close before. He had battled hard. But something had always gone wrong.

An injury. A crash. A bad race.

But not this time.

This time, Eli was more focused than ever. He trained harder. He pushed himself further. And as the 2020 Supercross season started, he was ready for battle.

The championship wasn't easy. He was racing against incredible riders like Ken Roczen, Cooper Webb, and Jason Anderson—some of the toughest Supercross racers in history.

But Eli wasn't afraid.

Race after race, he fought for every single point. He made bold passes. He took risks. He never backed down.

And then, just when things were going great—everything changed.

A global pandemic struck.

Races were postponed.

Stadiums emptied.

The world felt frozen in time.

For the first time in history, the Supercross season was put on hold. Nobody knew when—or if—the races would continue.

And Eli?

He had no choice but to wait.

For weeks, he trained alone, unsure if the season would ever return.

But when the races finally came back, something was different.

The fans were gone. The riders had to race in empty stadiums. There were no cheers, no crowds, no energy.

And for many riders, this was hard. Some struggled to stay focused. Some lost their momentum.

But not Eli.

Eli saw one thing—a championship waiting to be won.

And so, race after race, he fought harder than ever.

He battled through the strangest Supercross season in history.

And in the final round, in Salt Lake City, Utah, he crossed the finish line—as the champion.

He had done it.

Eli Tomac was officially the 2020 Supercross Champion.

It was a victory that meant everything.

He had waited years for this moment. He had come so close before. He had fought through every challenge, every setback, and every obstacle.

And now?

He was a Supercross Champion.

But Eli didn't stop there.

Because to stay at the top, a racer has to have something even more important than speed.

They have to have consistency and determination.

Now, what does that mean?

It means never getting comfortable.

It means waking up every single day, even after a big win, and saying:

"I have to train harder."

"I have to be better."

"I have to keep pushing."

Many riders win one big title and lose motivation. They get lazy. They stop training as hard. They think their job is done.

But not Eli.

He kept going.

He defended his titles.

He won more races.

He kept proving, year after year, that he wasn't just a great rider—he was one of the best ever.

And that?

That's what makes a true champion.

Chapter 7: The Rivalries and Comebacks

Eli Tomac's journey to becoming a motocross champion was not easy. It was filled with amazing victories, tough battles, and unforgettable races. But there was something else, something every great athlete has to face—injuries and setbacks.

Motocross is one of the most challenging sports in the world. Riders push their bikes to the limit, soaring over jumps, speeding through rough tracks, and making split-second decisions that could mean winning or crashing. The risks are huge, and the injuries can be serious. Eli knew this. Every rider did. But knowing the risks never stopped him from doing what he loved.

One of the worst moments of his career came in 2015. Eli was riding better than ever. He was one of the fastest riders on the track, battling for the 450cc Motocross Championship. Everything was going perfectly. Fans and experts believed this was his year. He had won the first five motos of the season—which means he had won every race so far. He was leading in points, and people thought he might dominate the entire year.

Then, disaster struck.

During the Thunder Valley National race in Colorado, Eli was leading. He was riding smoothly, looking strong. But in motocross, things can change in an instant. In the middle of the race, Eli lost control of his bike. He crashed—hard.

The crowd gasped. The announcers fell silent. Eli didn't get up right away. Something was wrong.

When the medical team rushed to help him, they discovered that both of his shoulders were injured. His left shoulder was dislocated, and his right shoulder was torn up badly. It was clear he couldn't finish the race. But worse than that, it was clear that his season was over.

A motocross rider needs strong arms and shoulders to control the bike. With both of Eli's shoulders damaged, there was no way he could keep racing. He needed surgery. He needed time to heal. And that meant sitting out for the rest of the championship.

It was heartbreaking. Eli had worked so hard to get to this moment. He was leading in points. He was ready to fight for his first 450cc title. But in one second, everything had changed. He had gone from the top of the championship standings to being out for the season.

For months, he couldn't race. Instead of riding his bike, he was doing physical therapy—slow, painful exercises to rebuild the strength in his shoulders. He watched from the sidelines as other riders competed for the championship he had been leading. It was one of the hardest times in his career.

But Eli Tomac is not the kind of person who gives up. He doesn't let setbacks stop him. He knew that he had two choices—stay down or get back up. And he chose to fight.

By the start of the 2016 season, he was back on the bike. His shoulders were healed, but he still had to prove that he was the same rider as before. Some people doubted him. They wondered if the injuries had slowed him down. They thought maybe he wouldn't be as strong, as fast, as fearless.

But Eli had something to show them.

That year, he started winning again. He wasn't just fast—he was better than before. He learned from his injury. He learned how to be smarter, tougher, and more focused. He didn't take anything for granted. He knew how quickly things could change, so he gave everything he had in every single race.

And then came one of the greatest comebacks wins in motocross history.

It was the 2017 Daytona Supercross. Daytona is one of the most famous and toughest Supercross races in the world. The track is long, rough, and built differently from every other Supercross track. It's one of the hardest races to win.

Eli started way behind. In the early laps, he wasn't even near the front. The leader, Jeremy Martin, had built a huge gap between himself and the rest of the riders. People thought there was no way Eli could catch him.

But Eli had other plans.

One by one, he started passing riders. He pushed his bike harder, found faster lines, and closed the gap. He was riding like a man on a mission. With just a few laps left, he had caught up to Martin. The two battled side by side.

And then, with a perfect move in the final laps, Eli passed Martin and took the lead.

The crowd erupted. Fans jumped out of their seats. Eli didn't just win—he made history.

That race proved something important. It showed that Eli never gives up. It showed that even when things look impossible, he finds a way to fight back.

And that wasn't his only legendary comeback win.

In 2018, at the Tampa Supercross, he had a terrible start. He was way behind. The leader had a huge gap ahead of him. But Eli refused to let that stop him. He rode harder, faster, and never stopped pushing.

One by one, he passed every single rider on the track.

And by the time the checkered flag waved, Eli Tomac had won again.

Again and again, he proved that he was a fighter.

No matter how many injuries, crashes, or bad starts he had, he always came back stronger.

This is why people called him a legendary rider. It wasn't just because he was fast. It wasn't just because he won races. It was because he never gave up.

Every time people thought Eli was out, he found a way to rise again.

Every time he faced a setback; he used it to become even better.

And that's what makes a true champion.

Chapter 8: Switching Teams

A New Chapter

Eli Tomac had spent years riding at the top of the motocross world. He had raced against the fastest riders, won huge championships, and become a fan favorite. But in the world of motocross, things are always changing. And in 2022, something big changed for Eli.

For years, Eli had raced for Kawasaki, one of the most powerful and famous motocross brands in the world. But then, he made a huge decision—he left Kawasaki and moved to Yamaha. It was a shocking move, something that nobody saw coming. But why did he do it? Why would a champion leave a team that had helped him win so many races?

To understand, we have to look at who Kawasaki and Yamaha are.

Kawasaki is one of the biggest motorcycle brands in the world. Their bikes are green, powerful, and built for speed. They had been with Eli for six years, helping him win races and championships. Together, Eli and Kawasaki had dominated the motocross world. They had won Supercross and Motocross titles, battled against the best riders, and built a strong partnership.

So why leave?

Because sometimes, even when things seem good, a rider knows they need a fresh start.

Eli had achieved everything with Kawasaki. He had won races, made history, and reached the top of the sport. But deep down, he felt like something was missing. He wanted a new challenge. He wanted a new experience. And Yamaha, another legendary motocross brand, gave him that opportunity.

Now, what is Yamaha?

Yamaha is another huge motorcycle brand, just like Kawasaki. Their bikes are blue, fast, and built to win. They had been competing against Kawasaki for years. In fact, many of Eli's biggest battles on the track had been against Yamaha riders.

But Yamaha had a problem. They hadn't won a Supercross title in years. They were still one of the best teams, but they needed a rider who could bring them back to the top. And that's where Eli came in.

Eli was one of the best riders in the world, and Yamaha wanted him to help them win again. So, in 2022, at the age of 29, Eli made the decision—he switched from Kawasaki to Yamaha.

It was a huge risk.

He had been comfortable with Kawasaki. He knew their bikes inside and out. He knew how the team worked, how the mechanics set up his bike, and how everything felt. But with Yamaha? Everything was new.

And that meant he had to learn everything all over again.

Now, some people might think, "Eli already knows how to ride a dirt bike. Why would he need to learn again?"

But here's the thing—not all bikes are the same.

The Yamaha bike was completely different from the Kawasaki bike. It handled differently. It felt different on the track. It reacted differently to jumps, turns, and bumps. Even the engine sound was different.

Eli had to retrain his brain.

He had to adjust his riding style.

He had to learn how to make this new bike work for him.

It was like learning how to race all over again.

At first, some people doubted him. They wondered if he had made a mistake. What if the Yamaha bike wasn't as good as his Kawasaki bike? What if he didn't feel comfortable? What if he couldn't win?

But Eli had one goal—to prove that he had made the right choice.

And when the 2022 Supercross season started, something incredible happened.

Eli didn't just adjust to the Yamaha bike—he dominated on it.

Race after race, he beat the competition.

He won in Anaheim. He won in Detroit. He won in Seattle.

And before long, he was leading the championship standings.

By the end of the 2022 Supercross season, Eli had done something amazing.

He won the Supercross Championship with Yamaha.

His first season with a brand-new team. A brand-new bike. A brand-new challenge.

And he had won it all.

It was one of the greatest moves in motocross history.

Eli had taken a huge risk, and it had paid off in the biggest way possible.

He had proven that it didn't matter what bike he rode—he was a champion, no matter what.

Chapter 9: Records, Achievements, and Legacy

Eli's Place in Motocross History

Eli Tomac's journey in motocross has been filled with challenges, victories, and moments that will be remembered forever. From the time he was a little boy, riding his first dirt bike, to the day he became a champion, he has shown the world what it means to never give up. But where does he stand among the greatest riders in history? What makes him special? Why will people still talk about him many years from now?

To understand Eli's place in motocross history, we have to look at what makes a legend. A legend is not just someone who wins races. A legend is someone who changes the sport. Someone who rides in a way that inspires people. Someone who never backs down, never quits, and always pushes the limits. That is exactly what Eli Tomac has done.

Motocross has had many great riders over the years. There was Ricky Carmichael, known as "The Greatest of All Time" because he won so many championships. There was Jeremy McGrath, the "King of Supercross," who set records that no one thought could ever be broken. There was James Stewart, one of the fastest riders ever, who could do things on a dirt bike that no one else could.

And then, there is Eli Tomac.

Eli has done something that not many riders have done—he has won in both Supercross and Motocross, proving that he can be the best in any kind of race. Some riders are good at Supercross, where they race in stadiums with huge jumps and tight turns. Some riders are better at Motocross, where they race on long outdoor tracks filled with hills and rough terrain. But Eli? He dominates both.

That is one of the reasons why people call him one of the greatest riders of all time.

But winning isn't just about speed. It's about determination. And Eli has had to fight harder than most to become a champion. He has battled injuries, crashes, and tough competitors. There were times when people doubted him, when they thought he might not be able to come back from an injury, when they wondered if he could win a championship.

But every time, he proved them wrong.

One of the things that makes Eli special is that he never gives up. He keeps pushing, keeps improving, and keeps finding ways to win. That's why he is a fan favorite. Kids and adults look up to him because he is not just fast—he is fearless.

People will always remember his incredible comeback wins, when he started a race in last place and still managed to pass every single rider and win. They will remember how he fought for his first Supercross championship, never giving up even when things got tough. They will remember the moment when he switched teams, took a huge risk, and still became a champion.

Not many riders can do what Eli has done. He has set records. He has won championship after championship. He has defeated some of the world's top riders. And he has done it all with heart, passion, and determination.

So where does Eli Tomac stand in motocross history?

He stands among the greatest riders of all time.

He stands as a champion.

He stands as a legend.

And most importantly, he stands as a rider who has inspired millions—not just with his speed, but with his spirit.

His career highlights

Eli Tomac's motocross career has been nothing short of amazing. From the moment he first sat on a dirt bike to the day he became a champion, he has given everything to the sport he loves. But what makes Eli one of the greatest riders in history? It's not just the races he's won—it's the records he's set and the history he's made.

Eli has raced for many years, and during that time, he has accomplished things that very few riders ever have. Some riders win a few races. Some riders win a championship or two. But Eli? He has done so much more. He has broken records, achieved things that only a handful of riders have ever done, and left behind a legacy that will be remembered forever.

One of Eli's biggest accomplishments was becoming one of the few riders in history to win both a Supercross and a Motocross championship. These are two very different types of racing, and winning in both shows that a rider is one of the best ever.

In 2017, 2018, and 2019, Eli won the AMA Pro Motocross Championship in the 450cc class. That meant that for three years, he was the fastest outdoor motocross rider in the world. He battled against the best, raced on the roughest tracks, and proved that he could conquer any challenge.

But he wasn't done.

In 2020, Eli finally won his first Supercross championship. This was something he had worked towards for years, and when he finally crossed the finish line as the champion, it was one of the greatest moments in his career. Supercross is one of the hardest championships to win because the races are short, fast, and intense. But Eli showed that he could handle the pressure and still come out on top.

Winning both Motocross and Supercross championships put Eli in a special group of riders—only a few in history have ever been able to do both.

But Eli didn't just win championships. He also set all-time records that will be remembered forever.

One of his most impressive records was his incredible comeback wins. There were races where Eli started near last place, way behind the leaders, and still managed to pass every single rider and win the race. Not many riders in history have been able to do that, and Eli did it multiple times.

Another amazing record was how many motos he won in a single season. In 2017, Eli won nine out of twelve races in the AMA Pro Motocross Championship. That means in almost every race, he was the first one to cross the finish line. It was one of the most dominant performances in motocross history.

Eli also became one of the winningest Supercross riders of all time. He joined the list of legends who have won the most races, proving that he is one of the best riders to ever compete.

But what makes Eli truly special isn't just the records or the championships. It's the way he raced. Every time he got on his bike, he gave everything he had. He didn't just ride to win—he rode to inspire.

Fans loved watching him because he was fearless. He could be far behind, in the worst conditions, facing the toughest competition, and he would still find a way to push forward and fight for victory.

And that's why his name will always be remembered in motocross history.

Eli Tomac didn't just win races—he became a legend.

A Hero for Young Riders

Eli Tomac has spent years racing through dirt tracks, flying over jumps, and battling against the fastest motocross riders in the world. He has won championships, set records, and proven that he is one of the best riders in history. But one of the most important things about Eli isn't just what he has done on the track—it's what he has done off the track.

Because Eli Tomac isn't just a motocross champion. He's a hero for young riders everywhere.

When Eli was a kid, he looked up to the best racers in the world. He watched them on TV, studied how they rode, and dreamed of one day becoming just like them. He wanted to race. He wanted to win. But more than anything, he wanted to be great.

Now, Eli is the one that young riders look up to. Kids all over the world watch him race and think, "I want to be like Eli

Tomac." They see how fast he is, how fearless he is, how he never gives up, and it inspires them.

Some kids ride their dirt bikes in their backyards, pretending they are Eli, imagining themselves zooming past other riders and winning championships. Some go to races and cheer for him, holding up signs that say "Go Eli!" and wearing his number on their shirts. And some, the ones who dream of racing one day, follow his journey closely, learning from everything he does.

Eli knows this. He knows that kids are watching. And that's why he always tries to be a great role model.

Being a role model isn't just about winning races. It's about showing kids how to work hard, stay focused, and never give up. It's about being someone they can look up to, not just for their speed, but for their heart.

Eli teaches young riders that success doesn't come overnight. It takes practice, patience, and determination. Every championship he has won came from years of hard work. He fell. He crashed. He lost races. But he always got back up. And that's a lesson every young rider can learn—that failing is part of the journey, but quitting is not.

Kids who follow Eli's career see that hard work pays off. They see that even a little boy from a small town in Colorado can grow up to be one of the best in the world. And that means that they can do it too.

Eli also inspires young riders by showing them how to stay humble. Even after winning so many races, he never brags. He never says he is better than anyone else. He respects his competitors. He thanks his team. He knows that motocross is not just about being fast—it's about being a good person too.

Another thing that makes Eli a hero for young riders is that he always takes time for his fans.

After races, he signs autographs, takes pictures, and talks to the kids who look up to him. He doesn't just rush away—he makes sure to connect with the people who support him.

And when young riders get the chance to meet him, it's something they will never forget.

Some kids have waited for hours just to shake his hand. And when they do, they leave with a huge smile, feeling even more excited to chase their own dreams.

Eli also gives back to the sport by helping young racers who are just starting out. He supports amateur races, encourages kids to follow their passion, and reminds them that no matter how hard things get, they should never stop believing in themselves.

His story is proof that with hard work and dedication, anything is possible.

That's why Eli Tomac is not just a champion.

He is a hero for the next generation.

A hero for every kid who dreams of racing.

A hero who shows that chasing your dreams is always worth it.

Chapter 10: Life Beyond the Track

Eli Tomac is known all around the world as one of the fastest motocross riders ever. He has won huge championships, broken records, and battled against the best riders in history. But when he takes off his helmet and steps away from the race track, who is Eli Tomac? What is he like when he is not speeding through dirt tracks, flying over jumps, and fighting for victories?

Many people see Eli as a fierce competitor—strong, focused, and fearless on the track. But when he's not racing, he is just a regular guy who loves his family, enjoys spending time outdoors, and believes in helping young riders chase their dreams. He is more than just a champion—he is a husband, a father, an adventurer, and an inspiration.

Eli's life changed in an incredible way when he met Jessica Steiner, the woman who would later become his wife. Jessica had been with him through some of his most important career moments—the big races, the championships, the challenges, and the victories. She supported him when things were tough and celebrated with him when he stood on top of the podium.

In November 2021, after years of being together, Eli and Jessica got married. It was a beautiful day filled with love, family, and happiness. Even though Eli had already won many motocross titles, this was one of the biggest moments of his life. Being a champion on the track was important to him, but having a loving family was even more special.

Not long after their wedding, something even more amazing happened—Eli became a dad!

In April 2021, Eli and Jessica welcomed their first child, a baby girl named Lev Loe Tomac. Becoming a father was a new adventure for Eli, one that was different from racing but just as exciting. Holding his baby girl for the first time was a moment he would never forget.

And then, in September 2023, their family grew even bigger! Eli and Jessica had their second child, a baby boy. Now, Eli wasn't just a champion motocross rider—he was also a dad of two!

Even though racing was his career, his family was his greatest victory.

Being a father changed Eli's life. Racing was still important, but now, when he came home after long days of training, there was something even more special waiting for him— his children. He loved spending time with them, watching them grow, and being the best dad he could be. Even though they were still young, Eli knew that one day, they might want to ride dirt bikes too. Maybe they would follow in his footsteps, or maybe they would choose their own dreams. Either way, Eli was ready to support them just like his own parents had supported him.

Outside of motocross and family life, Eli has many hobbies and interests. He is not just about racing—he loves being outdoors and enjoys adventure, nature, and physical challenges.

One of his biggest hobbies is mountain biking. This is not surprising, since his dad, John Tomac, was a world-famous mountain biker. Even though motocross and mountain biking are different, they both require strength, balance, and quick thinking. Eli loves riding through trails, climbing steep hills, and feeling the thrill of the ride—just like he does in motocross, but without an engine!

Another thing Eli enjoys is hunting. Some people might think hunting is just about chasing animals, but for Eli, it's about something much deeper. It's about patience, skill, and respect for nature. He enjoys spending quiet time outdoors, learning about the land, and challenging himself in different ways.

Eli also enjoys spending time with animals. On his family's property in Colorado, there are often horses, dogs, and other animals around. He believes in caring for them, respecting them, and enjoying the simple moments of life.

Even though motocross takes up most of his time, he always finds moments to enjoy the things that make him happy. Whether it's riding a bicycle up a mountain, sitting outside in the fresh air, or playing with his kids, Eli believes that life is about more than just winning—it's about doing what you love.

One of the most special things about Eli Tomac is how much he gives back to the motocross community. He knows that many young kids dream of becoming riders just like him, and he wants to help them on their journey.

Eli understands how difficult it can be to start motocross. Dirt bikes, gear, and race fees can be expensive, and not every kid has the chance to train and compete. That's why Eli does his best to support young riders in any way he can.

One way he gives back is by supporting amateur motocross events. He knows that these races are where future stars are born, just like he once raced in them as a kid. He sometimes attends these events, cheers for young racers, and even gives advice. When kids see Eli watching them, it makes them feel excited, motivated, and proud.

Eli also takes time to meet his fans. After races, he stays to sign autographs, take pictures, and talk to the kids who look up to him. He knows that even a short conversation or a simple high-five can mean the world to a young fan. Some kids dream about meeting their favorite rider, and when they finally get to shake Eli's hand, they never forget it.

He has also worked with brands and organizations that help young racers get started in motocross. Not every kid has a dirt bike, and not every family can afford to buy one. Eli helps by working with companies that donate bikes, gear, and training equipment to kids who need them. This gives more kids a chance to ride and follow their motocross dreams.

Eli's biggest message to young riders is simple—never give up. He knows that everyone falls, crashes, and struggles at first, but that doesn't mean they should quit. Every champion starts as a beginner. Every winner has lost races before. The key is to keep trying, keep believing, and keep pushing forward.

Eli Tomac is not just a motocross champion—he is an inspiration to kids everywhere. He has shown that with hard work, dedication, and passion, anything is possible. He has proven that being a champion is not just about winning races but about staying humble, being kind, and helping others.

Now, young riders everywhere look up to Eli, not just because he is fast, but because he is a great role model. He teaches kids that dreams don't come true overnight, but if they work hard and never stop believing, they can achieve anything.

And that's why Eli Tomac is more than just a racer—he is a hero, on and off the track.

Chapter 11: The Future of Eli Tomac

Eli Tomac has spent years thrilling fans, battling against the best riders in the world, and proving time and time again that he is one of the greatest motocross racers in history. He has raced on the toughest tracks, soared over the biggest jumps, and pushed himself to limits that most people could only imagine. He has faced fierce competitors, experienced the highest victories and the hardest falls, but no matter what, he has always gotten back up and fought even harder. His journey has been one of dedication, strength, and determination, but as with every great athlete, there comes a time when people start to wonder—what's next?

For years, Eli has been at the top of the sport, winning races and championships in both Supercross and Motocross. He has beaten records, made history, and inspired young riders all over the world. But motocross is a demanding sport, one that requires intense training, sharp focus, and the ability to recover quickly from crashes and injuries. As time goes on, many wonder how long Eli will continue racing at such a high level and what he will do when he eventually steps away from competition.

Will he keep racing for several more years? Will he retire and focus on other things? Or will he take on a brand-new challenge? These are the questions that fans ask as they watch his incredible career continue to unfold.

Eli has never been the type of rider to rush into decisions. He loves motocross and has dedicated his entire life to it, but he also knows that every career eventually comes to an end. Many riders continue competing into their mid-30s, while others decide to retire earlier to pursue new adventures. As of now, Eli is still one of the fastest riders on the track, still capable of winning races, and still proving that he is among the best.

However, one thing is certain—when Eli Tomac does decide to step away from full-time racing, his impact on the sport will last forever.

Motocross is a sport that is constantly changing, with new riders coming in and old legends retiring, but only a few racers truly leave their mark in a way that changes the sport forever. Eli is one of those rare athletes. His influence goes beyond just the championships he has won. He has redefined what it means to be a racer—someone who never backs down, never quits, and always gives their best.

One of the biggest ways Eli has changed motocross is through his incredible ability to make comeback wins. Many times in his career, he has started races far behind the leaders, sometimes even in last place, and yet he has found a way to charge forward, passing one rider after another until he crossed the finish line first. This kind of determination and ability to fight back has inspired many young riders, teaching them that no race is ever over until the checkered flag waves.

Eli's racing style has also influenced a new generation of riders. He is known for his aggressive yet smart approach, taking bold risks but always keeping control of his bike. His fearless attitude on the track has made races more exciting, keeping fans on the edge of their seats, waiting to see what he will do next.

He has also shown the world that switching teams and bikes doesn't have to be a disadvantage. When he moved from Kawasaki to Yamaha, some people wondered if he would struggle with the transition. Instead, he adapted quickly, adjusted to his new bike, and won a championship in his first season with Yamaha. This showed younger riders that change can be a good thing and that success is possible no matter what challenges you face.

But perhaps the most important impact Eli has had on motocross is the way he has inspired kids. Many young riders dream of becoming professionals one day, and when they watch Eli race, they see someone who has worked hard, stayed focused, and never given up—even when things got tough. He has become a hero for many kids, not just because he is fast, but because he is determined, humble, and always willing to help others.

So, what can young riders and fans learn from Eli Tomac's journey? What lessons can they take from his career and apply to their own lives?

One of the biggest lessons from Eli's story is hard work pays off. When Eli was a little boy, he wasn't the fastest rider right away. He didn't just wake up one day as a champion. Instead, he practiced every day, listened to his dad's advice, and trained harder than anyone else. This teaches kids that success doesn't come overnight—it takes time, effort, and patience.

Another lesson from Eli's journey is never give up, no matter how tough things get. Eli has had injuries that could have ended his career, races where he started in last place, and moments where things didn't go as planned. But did he quit? No. Every time something knocked him down, he got back up and tried again. This is an important lesson for kids because life is full of challenges, but those who keep going and never stop believing in themselves will always have a chance to succeed.

Eli has also shown that staying humble and respecting others is just as important as winning. Even though he has won many championships, he doesn't brag or act like he is better than anyone else. He always thanks his team, respects his competitors, and takes time to meet fans, sign autographs, and inspire the next generation.

So, what's next for Eli Tomac? Will he continue racing for more years, chasing even more championships? Will he step away from full-time racing and focus on something new? Will he take on a different role in motocross, perhaps as a coach or a mentor for young riders? Nobody knows for sure, but one thing is certain—his legacy will never be forgotten.

Whether he keeps racing, retires, or explores new challenges, Eli has already done more than enough to secure his place in motocross history. He has inspired riders, broken records, and left an impact that will last for generations. He has shown the world what it means to work hard, believe in yourself, and never stop chasing your dreams.

And for every young rider out there, dreaming of one day being a champion, Eli's story is proof that if you are willing to put in the work, stay focused, and never give up, anything is possible.

🏁 Fun Facts About Eli Tomac 🏁

1. **Eli Tomac was born on November 14, 1992, in Cortez, Colorado.** That means he grew up surrounded by mountains, trails, and lots of places to ride!

2. **His dad, John Tomac, was a professional mountain bike racer!** His dad was a world

champion in cycling, so Eli grew up around bikes his whole life.

3. **Eli rode his first dirt bike when he was just three years old!** While most kids were learning to ride bicycles, Eli was already twisting the throttle on a mini dirt bike.

4. **His first-ever motocross race was when he was just 7 years old!** And from that moment on, he knew he wanted to race for the rest of his life.

5. **Eli won his first professional motocross race in his very first try!** In 2010, at 17 years old, he shocked everyone by winning his first pro race at the Hangtown Motocross Classic.

6. **He became the first rookie in history to win his first 250cc Pro Motocross race!** No one had ever done that before—talk about a legendary start!

7. **Eli has raced for two of the biggest motocross teams in the world: Kawasaki and Yamaha.** He raced for Kawasaki for years before switching to Yamaha in 2022.

8. **His racing number is #3.** Every motocross rider has a special number, and Eli picked #3 because it was his favorite!

9. **Eli Tomac is known for his crazy fast comeback wins!** He has started races in last place and still fought his way to first place by the end!

10. **He won his first Supercross championship in 2020!** After years of hard work, he finally achieved his dream and became the Supercross champion.

11. **Eli has won multiple AMA Motocross Championships.** He dominated the outdoor tracks in 2017, 2018, and 2019.

12. **He is known for his fearless riding style.** Fans love watching Eli because he races with full speed and never holds back!

13. **One of his favorite hobbies is mountain biking.** When he's not racing dirt bikes, he's riding mountain bikes just like his dad used to.

14. **He loves spending time outdoors.** Whether it's hiking, riding bikes, or just being in nature, Eli enjoys life outside of racing.

15. **Eli is married to Jessica Steiner.** They got married in November 2021 after many years together.

16. **He is a proud dad of two kids.** He has a daughter named Lev Loe, born in 2021, and a son born in 2023.

17. **Eli grew up on a big ranch in Colorado.** He had plenty of space to ride, practice, and enjoy the outdoors.

18. **He loves animals!** He has dogs and enjoys being around horses and other animals on his property.

19. **Eli's favorite Supercross race is Daytona.** He has won at Daytona multiple times and always puts on a great show!

20. **He once won a race by passing 21 riders!** In the 2018 Tampa Supercross, Eli started at the back but passed everyone to take the win.

21. **Eli is one of the fastest riders in history.** His lap times are often some of the best in the world.

22. **He rides a Yamaha YZ450F.** This is the bike he uses in the 450cc class, and it's one of the most powerful motocross bikes ever!

23. **His bike can go over 80 miles per hour!** That's faster than the majority of highway vehicles!

24. **He trains really hard to stay in shape.** Motocross racing is physically demanding, so he lifts weights, runs, and does special workouts.

25. **Eli wears custom motocross gear.** His jerseys, pants, and helmets are specially designed for him and have his name and number on them.

26. **His helmets are super high-tech.** They are designed to protect his head in case of a crash and are made from lightweight but super strong materials.

27. **Eli's race bike is worth more than $50,000!** It is custom-built with the best parts and technology to help him go faster.

28. **He gives back to young racers.** Eli donates gear, supports amateur races, and helps kids who want to get into motocross.

29. **He has thousands of fans all over the world!** People from different countries cheer for Eli and love watching him race.

30. **Eli Tomac never gives up!** No matter how tough a race gets, he always pushes forward and never stops believing in himself.

🏍 Fun Facts About Motorcycles to Blow Your Mind! 🏍

1. **The first motorcycle was built in 1885!** A German inventor named **Gottlieb Daimler** built a wooden bike with an engine, and it was the first motorcycle ever!

2. **The fastest motorcycle in the world can go over 400 mph!** The **Dodge Tomahawk** is a futuristic motorcycle that can reach speeds faster than some airplanes!

3. **Some motorcycles are so loud they can be heard from miles away!** The sound of a motorcycle's engine can travel super far, especially on open roads.

4. **The world's biggest motorcycle is 16 feet long!** This giant bike was built in Italy and is taller than most cars!

5. **The smallest motorcycle in the world is shorter than a ruler!** It is called the **Smalltoe**, and it's only 10 inches tall—tiny enough to fit in a backpack!

6. **Motorcycles are faster than most cars!** A high-performance motorcycle can accelerate from **0 to 60 mph in just 2 seconds!**

7. **Some motorcycles can ride on water!** There are specially designed dirt bikes that can go across lakes and rivers if they are fast enough!

8. **Motorcycle tires are not completely round!** They are curved to help riders lean into turns and keep their balance at high speeds.

9. **The longest motorcycle jump ever was over 300 feet!** A stunt rider named Robbie Maddison set the record by jumping the length of a football field!

10. **Motorcycle engines can last longer than car engines!** With the right care, some bikes can be ridden for **hundreds of thousands of miles**!

11. **The most expensive motorcycle in the world costs over $11 million!** It's called the **Neiman Marcus Limited Edition Fighter**, and it looks like something from a superhero movie!

12. **Some motorcycles have three wheels!** These are called **trikes**, and they are great for riders who want more stability.

13. **In some countries, police use motorcycles to chase bad guys!** Police motorcycles are super fast and can weave through traffic easily.

14. **There is a motorcycle that transforms into a jet ski!** It's called the **Gibbs Biski**, and it can ride on both land and water!

15. **Some motorcycles don't even need gas!** Electric motorcycles run on batteries and can be **super quiet and super fast**.

16. **Motorcycle racing is one of the most dangerous sports in the world!** Riders can go over **200 mph**, lean their bikes nearly sideways, and still control them!

17. **In some places, motorcycles are used as taxis!** In countries like Thailand and Nigeria, people ride on the back of motorcycles instead of cars to get around quickly.

18. **Some motorcycles can go backward!** While most motorcycles only move forward, some special stunt bikes can be modified to go in reverse.

19. **Dirt bikes are different from regular motorcycles!** They have special tires, lighter frames, and strong suspensions to handle jumping and rough terrain.

20. **The longest motorcycle ride in history was over 500,000 miles!** A man named **Emilio Scotto** rode

his motorcycle across **214 countries** over 10 years—talk about an adventure!

Motorcycles are **amazing machines** built for speed, adventure, and fun! Whether they're used for racing, jumping, or just cruising down the road, they are some of the coolest vehicles ever made! 🏍️ 💨

Eli's Favorite Tracks and Races

Eli Tomac has raced on many tracks across the world, but there are some that stand out as his absolute favorites—tracks where he feels the fastest, the strongest, and the most in control of his bike. These are the places where he has had some of his greatest victories, battled some of the toughest riders, and made motocross history. Every racer has certain tracks where they just seem to shine, where everything comes together perfectly, and they feel unstoppable. For Eli, these tracks are more than just dirt and jumps—they are places where his greatest memories have been made, his biggest battles have been fought, and his most incredible wins have taken place.

One of Eli's all-time favorite tracks is Daytona International Speedway, home to one of the most famous

Supercross races in the world—the Daytona Supercross. Daytona is unlike any other Supercross track. Most Supercross races take place inside stadiums, where the tracks are built on flat ground with sharp turns and steep jumps. But Daytona is different. The track is built on the infield of a huge NASCAR speedway, and it is longer, rougher, and much more challenging than other Supercross tracks. The dirt is soft and deep, which makes it much harder to ride through, and because the track is outdoors, the weather can change everything. Some years, the track has been muddy, making it slippery and difficult to control the bike, and other years, it has been dry and sandy, making it tough to get traction.

Eli loves racing at Daytona because it requires a combination of speed, strength, and endurance. It is not just about who is the fastest—it is about who can handle the roughest conditions and stay strong all the way to the finish line. Eli has won at Daytona multiple times, and every time he does, it proves that he is one of the best Supercross riders in history. One of his greatest wins at Daytona came in 2017, when he put on a performance that left the crowd speechless. He started the race behind the leaders, but as the laps went on, he charged through the pack, passing riders one by one until he took the lead. The crowd went wild as he pulled ahead, hitting every jump perfectly and navigating every turn with precision. By the time he crossed the finish line, he had created a huge gap between himself and the second-place rider. It was one of the most dominant victories Daytona had ever seen, and it cemented Eli's reputation as a rider who thrives in the toughest conditions.

Another track where Eli has made history is Thunder Valley Motocross Park, located in his home state of Colorado. Thunder Valley is special to Eli because it is where he grew up. As a kid, he would watch races there, dreaming of one day competing against the best riders in the world. When he finally got the chance to race at Thunder Valley as a professional, it was a dream come true. Racing in front of his home crowd, with thousands of fans cheering him on, made it even more special.

One of his best races at Thunder Valley came in 2018, when he won in dominating fashion. The track, which is set at a high altitude in the Rocky Mountains, makes it harder for riders because the air is thinner, meaning the bikes don't have as much power, and the riders get tired more easily. But Eli, being from Colorado, was used to the altitude and knew how to handle it better than anyone else. That year, he took the lead early in the race and never looked back. He flew over the jumps, powered through the turns, and put together one of the most flawless rides of his career. The fans erupted in cheers as he crossed the finish line, celebrating not just a race win but a victory in his home state.

Another legendary track where Eli has had incredible success is RedBud MX, one of the most iconic motocross tracks in the United States. RedBud is famous for its huge jumps, fast straights, and massive crowds of excited fans. Every year, thousands of people pack into the track, waving American flags, chanting "RedBuuuud!" and cheering for their favorite riders. The energy at RedBud is unlike any other race, and Eli feeds off that energy every time he competes there.

In 2019, Eli had one of his most thrilling wins at RedBud. The race was intense from the very start, with several riders battling for the lead. Eli got off to a strong start, but the competition was fierce. For most of the race, he was in a heated battle with another top rider, Ken Roczen, who refused to back down. The two riders swapped positions multiple times, passing each other back and forth, with neither willing to give an inch. The crowd was on its feet, roaring as the battle unfolded. With just a few laps to go, Eli made his move, finding the perfect line to take the lead for good. He charged ahead, pushing his bike to its limit, and when he crossed the finish line in first place, he had once again proved why he was one of the best in the world.

Another unforgettable race for Eli was at Southwick Motocross Park, a track known for having the deepest, softest sand in motocross. Riding in sand is one of the most difficult challenges in motocross because the bike sinks into the ground, making it much harder to control. Some riders struggle at Southwick, but Eli thrives in the sand. He knows how to ride through the deep ruts, keep his speed up, and power through the rough terrain.

In 2016, he put on one of the best rides of his career at Southwick. The race started with another rider taking the early lead, but Eli didn't panic. He stayed patient, waiting for the right moment to make his move. As the race went on, he started picking up speed, riding smoother and faster than anyone else. With just a few laps to go, he finally made his move, passing the leader with an incredible burst of speed. From that moment on, he controlled the race, gliding through the sand like it was nothing, and taking one of the most impressive wins of the season.

One of the most legendary races of Eli's career happened at Unadilla MX, a track that has been around for decades and is known for its rough, challenging terrain. In 2017, Eli had one of his most unforgettable battles at Unadilla. The race was full of mud, rain, and unpredictable conditions, making it one of the toughest events of the year. Many riders struggled, slipping and sliding in the mud, but Eli thrived in the chaos.

He started the race mid-pack, but as the conditions got worse, he got faster. While other riders were struggling to keep their bikes upright, Eli was charging forward, passing riders one after another. By the final few laps, he had worked his way into the lead, and when he crossed the finish line, completely covered in mud, he had pulled off one of the most incredible wins of his career.

These are just a few of the many tracks where Eli Tomac has made history. Each one is special in its own way, whether it's the challenging sand of Southwick, the electric atmosphere of RedBud, the high altitude of Thunder Valley, or the legendary Daytona Supercross. Eli has proven that he can win anywhere, under any conditions, and against the toughest competition.

For kids who dream of one day racing like Eli, these tracks are more than just places to ride—they are battlefields where champions are made. Eli's incredible performances on these tracks have shown that with hard work, determination, and a never-give-up attitude, anything is possible. Whether he is racing in the deep sand, high in the mountains, or on one of the roughest tracks in the sport, Eli always finds a way to shine. And that is why he is one of the greatest riders motocross has ever seen.

🏍️ Motocross Terms Explained for Young Readers! 🏍️

Motocross has its own special language, filled with exciting words that every young rider should know! If you want to understand how motocross riders talk, here is a **fun and easy-to-understand glossary** that explains some of the most common motocross and motorcycle terms. Get ready to **learn the lingo of the dirt bike world!**

🔧 Bike & Gear Terms

- **Dirt Bike** – A special motorcycle made for off-road racing. Unlike street motorcycles, dirt bikes have knobby tires and strong suspensions to handle rough terrain.

- **Throttle** – The part of the bike that controls the speed. Riders twist the throttle on the right handlebar to make the bike go faster!

- **Clutch** – A lever on the left handlebar that helps change gears. Riders pull the clutch to shift smoothly.

- **Brakes** – The controls that **slow down or stop** the bike. The front brake is on the right handlebar, and the back brake is near the right footpeg.

- **Suspension** – The **shock absorbers** on a dirt bike that make landing jumps smoother and help riders handle bumpy tracks.

- **Knobby Tires** – The special tires on a dirt bike that have deep treads (bumps) to **grip the dirt and prevent slipping**.

- **Exhaust** – The pipe that lets out smoke and sound from the engine. A loud "braaap" sound comes from the exhaust when a rider revs their bike!

- **Helmet** – The most important piece of safety gear! Riders wear helmets to **protect their heads in case of a crash**.

- **Goggles** – Special glasses that protect a rider's eyes from **mud, dust, and flying rocks** during a race.

- **Jersey & Pants** – The special **clothes motocross riders wear**, made from strong but lightweight material to keep them safe and comfortable.

- **Gloves** – Worn to **protect a rider's hands** and give them a better grip on the handlebars.

- **Boots** – Tough boots that **protect a rider's feet, ankles, and legs** while riding.

⚑ Racing & Track Terms

- **Track** – The special course where motocross races happen! Tracks have **jumps, turns, hills, and rough sections**.

- **Start Gate** – The metal gate at the beginning of a race. When the gate drops, the race begins!

- **Holeshot** – The rider who **gets to the first turn first** after the race starts. Getting the holeshot is a big advantage in a race!

- **Lap** – One full ride around the track. Most motocross races have **multiple laps** before the winner is decided.

- **Moto** – A motocross race is called a **moto**. Most motocross events have **two motos**, and the rider with the best combined results wins.

- **Checkered Flag** – The black and white flag that **means the race is over**. The first rider to cross the finish line when the checkered flag waves is the winner!

- **Heat Race** – A **short race before the final race** to determine who moves on to compete for the championship.

- **Main Event** – The **final race of the night** in Supercross, where the top riders compete for victory.

- **Podium** – The stage where the top three riders **celebrate their win** and receive their trophies.

⚒ Riding & Jumping Terms

- **Whoops** – A series of **small bumps** that riders have to **bounce over really fast**.

- **Tabletop** – A type of jump that is flat on top, **like a table**. Riders try to clear the whole tabletop by flying over it.

- **Triple Jump** – A massive jump where a rider **jumps over three sections** of the track in one leap.

- **Berm** – A **raised bank of dirt** on the edge of a turn that helps riders lean and go around corners faster.

- **Scrub** – A cool trick where a rider **leans the bike sideways in the air** to stay lower and land quicker.

- **Whip** – A trick where a rider **turns the bike sideways in the air and then straightens it before landing**. It looks super cool!

- **Wheelie** – When a rider **lifts the front wheel off the ground** while still riding on the back wheel.

- **Endo** – A stunt where the **back wheel comes off the ground, and the rider balances on the front wheel** for a short time.

🔥 Racing & Riding Styles

- **Factory Rider** – A professional rider who **races for an official team** like Yamaha, Honda, or Kawasaki. These riders get the best bikes, gear, and support from the team.

- **Privateer** – A racer who **doesn't have a factory team** and competes using their own bike and support.

- **Pin It!** – A fun way of saying **"go as fast as possible"**!

- **Braap!** – The sound a dirt bike makes, and also what riders say when they're having fun riding!

- **Rubbing is Racing** – A funny way of saying that **bumping into other riders is just part of racing**!

- **Full Send** – When a rider **goes all out, jumps as far as possible, and gives everything they have in a race**.

- **DNF** – Stands for **"Did Not Finish"**—this means a rider had to stop a race before the end because of a crash or bike problem.

- **Fastest Lap** – The rider who completes **one lap in the shortest time** during the race.

- **Tearing Up the Track** – A way of saying that **a rider is going super fast and dominating the race**!

Fun Motocross Slang & Sayings

- **Eat Dirt** – When a rider crashes and falls into the dirt.

- **Ghost Ride** – When a rider jumps off their bike and lets it keep rolling without them!

- **Lapper** – A slower rider who gets **lapped** by the faster riders.

- **Riding on the Edge** – When a rider is pushing their limits and **going as fast as possible without crashing**.

- **Tight Battle** – When two or more riders are super close to each other and **fighting hard for the lead**.

- **Roost** – The dirt and rocks that fly up when a rider **spins their back tire**. If you're behind another rider, watch out for roost!

🏍 Now You Speak Motocross! 🏍

Now that you know these **awesome motocross words**, you can **talk like a real rider**! The next time you watch a race, you'll understand what's happening when the riders **hit the whoops, battle for the holeshot, send a massive**

whip, and fight for the checkered flag! Whether you're riding a dirt bike, cheering for your favorite racer, or just having fun learning about motocross, these words will help you feel like a **real motocross expert!** 🏁 🔥 👉

CONCLUSION

Eli Tomac's journey is one of speed, strength, and determination. From a little boy riding his first dirt bike in the open fields of Colorado to becoming one of the greatest motocross racers of all time, his story is proof that dreams really do come true if you work hard enough. He has raced on the toughest tracks, battled against the best riders in history, won incredible championships, and made motocross history in ways that will be remembered forever.

But Eli's story is more than just about winning races. It is a story about **never giving up, believing in yourself, and pushing through even when things get tough**. Every champion has challenges, and Eli faced plenty—injuries that could have ended his career, races where he started in last place, and moments where everything seemed to go wrong. But what made him different from so many others is that he never let those struggles stop him. Instead, he used every challenge as fuel to come back stronger, faster, and more determined than ever.

Throughout his career, Eli has shown that being a champion is not just about speed—it's also about **heart**. He has become a hero to young riders around the world, inspiring them not just with his victories, but with his attitude. He never brags, never looks down on his competitors, and always respects the sport. He takes time for his fans, signs autographs for kids, and encourages the next generation of racers to chase their dreams.

Eli Tomac is proof that **hard work pays off**. When he was a kid, he wasn't the fastest rider in the world. He had to practice, train, and dedicate himself to improving every single day. He didn't become a champion overnight—he became a champion by **putting in the work, staying focused, and never quitting**. And that is a lesson that any kid—whether they dream of racing dirt bikes or doing something else—can learn from.

But what's next for Eli Tomac? Will he continue to race for many more years, breaking even more records? Will he retire and focus on new adventures? Or will he take on a new role, helping young riders become champions just like him? Nobody knows for sure, but one thing is certain—**his legacy will live on forever**.

No matter what happens next, Eli has already **left his mark on motocross**. His incredible comeback wins, fearless racing style, and never-give-up attitude have changed the sport forever. He has inspired kids all over the world to get on their bikes, twist the throttle, and chase their own dreams.

So, whether you are a young rider dreaming of one day becoming a motocross star, or just a fan who loves the excitement of racing, remember the story of Eli Tomac. Remember that success comes to those who **never stop believing in themselves**. Remember that even the best riders in the world started as beginners. And most importantly, remember that if you work hard, stay focused, and never give up—**you can conquer any challenge, just like Eli did.**

Eli Tomac **was once just a kid with a dream**. But through passion, dedication, and determination, he became **The Boy Who Conquered the Dirt**. And now, his story will inspire young racers for generations to come. 🏁 🏍️ 🔥

Made in the USA
Coppell, TX
09 March 2025

46889926R00069